With Blessings:

_____

To

_____

From

_____

Date

"*It's a Good Day When* is a message of hope, steeped in the truth of God's Word, against the stunning backdrop of His creation. Robbi Cary pens a much-needed message that God is for us in each and every day of our lives and 'psalmist with a camera' Patricia Hunter's stunning photographs draw readers closer to God. This is a book to be savored—and shared."

　　—**Beth K. Vogt**, author, *Wish You Were Here*

"I love *It's a Good Day!* It's a warm fuzzy hug wrapping its arms around you on a bad day and a shield against discouragement in longer trials."

　　—**Lynne Pritchett**

"I was immediately captured by Patricia's ability to capture shutters full of wonder."

　　—**Patsy Clairmont**, author, *Stained Glass Hearts*

"Patricia Hunter is a gold miner with a camera. She unearths the light of Christ . . . and offers up pure nuggets of glory with her every shutter click. Encounter her and you will have struck it even richer in Christ."

　　—**Ann Voskamp**, author, *One Thousand Gifts*

No Matter What,
It's a Good Day When

FINDING BLESSINGS IN DIFFICULT DAYS

Robbi Cary / Photographs by Patricia Hunter

Blessings & grace,
Robbi
2 Peter 1: 2-11
Go make it a good day!

Hilltop House Publishing, Fort Myers, Florida

Unless otherwise noted, all quotations are from THE HOLY BIBLE, NEW
INTERNATIONAL VERSION®, NIV® [1984]. Copyright © 1973, 1978, 1984, 2011 by
Biblica, Inc.™ Used by permission. All rights reserved worldwide.

Scripture quotations from The Message. Copyright © by Eugene H. Peterson 1993,
1994, 1995, 1996, 2000, 2001, 2002. Used by permission of NavPress Publishing
Group.

Scriptures quotations from the New King James Version (NKJV). Copyright © 1982
by Thomas Nelson, Inc. Used by permission. All rights reserved.

Scripture quotations from the Holy Bible, New Living Translation (NLT).
Copyright © 1996, 2004, 2007 by Tyndale House Foundation. Used by permission
of Tyndale House Publishers, Inc., Carol Stream, Illinois 60188. All rights
reserved.

Scripture quotations from The Holy Bible, English Standard Version® (ESV®).
Copyright © 2001 by Crossway, a publishing ministry of Good News Publishers.
Used by permission. All rights reserved.

Scriptures quotations noted (KJV) are taken from the King James Version
(public domain).

ISBN 978-0-9893754-0-5
Library of Congress Control Number: 2013957903
Printed in the United States
Book design and production by BW&A Books, Inc.

Dear Friend,

If you are having a difficult time, our hearts and prayers go out to you. In our own lives—especially in difficult days—we have discovered and experienced that God is good and has good plans for us. We continue to see that the more we seek Him and open ourselves up to Him, the more we experience His goodness.

If you have questions and doubts about God's goodness and intentions, that's okay—we hope you will find this book helpful. May God bless you as you honestly seek Him and turn to Him, no matter what your circumstances.

Love,

Robbi and Patricia

No matter what your day holds—
bumps, bruises, or even a day filled with trials,
it's a good day
when you've seen a glimpse
of God's glory, power,
and goodness.

The heavens declare the glory of God.
—Psalm 19:1 NKJV

For since the creation of the world God's invisible qualities—His eternal power and divine nature—have been clearly seen.
—Romans 1:20

Even on a day heavy with burdens,
it's a good day
when you've been touched
by God's tenderness.

A bruised reed He will not break . . . says God the LORD, Who created the heavens and stretched them out, Who spread forth the earth and that which comes from it, Who gives breath to the people on it, And spirit to those who walk on it.
—Isaiah 42:3,5 NKJV

He raises up the poor from the dust; he lifts the needy from the ash heap.
—1 Samuel 2:8 ESV

It's a good day when you know that God
provides proof and evidence
for all He wants to show us
and He calls us to examine
His extraordinary promises and their fulfillment.

This [great] salvation, which was first announced by the Lord, was confirmed to us . . . God also testified to it by signs, wonders and various miracles.
    —Hebrews 2:3–4

He has given proof of this to all men by raising [Christ Jesus] from the dead.
    —Acts 17:31

"I am GOD, the only God you've had or ever will have—incomparable, irreplaceable—From the very beginning telling you what the ending will be, All along letting you in on what is going to happen, Assuring you, 'I'm in this for the long haul.'"
    —Isaiah 46:9–10 The Message

It's a good day when you know
that God is a God
of powerful promises.
He is a God of His Word.

The LORD is faithful to all his promises.
—Psalm 145:13

*For no matter how many promises God has made, they are "Yes" in
Christ. And so through him the "Amen" is spoken by us to the glory of
God.*
—2 Corinthians 1:20

It's a good day when you know
that God offers mercy,
forgiveness,
and reconciliation,
and you accept and embrace
these gifts every day.

The faithful love of the LORD never ends! His mercies never cease.
Great is his faithfulness; his mercies begin afresh each morning.
   —Lamentations 3:22–23 NLT

I tell you the truth, whoever hears my word and believes him who sent
me has eternal life and will not be condemned; he has crossed over from
death to life.
   —John 5:24

It's a good and miraculous day
when you seek God
and He enables you to see
and do
what you never could have imagined possible.

Now to him who is able to do far more abundantly than all that we ask or think, according to the power at work within us, to him be glory.
    —Ephesians 3:20–21 ESV

Do not be anxious about anything, but in everything by prayer and supplication with thanksgiving let your requests be made known to God.
    —Philippians 4:6 ESV

Jesus looked at them and said, "With man this is impossible, but with God all things are possible."
    —Matthew 19:26 ESV

It's a good day when you know that,
regardless of your circumstances,
you are deeply loved by God.

How priceless is your unfailing love! Both high and low among men find refuge in the shadow of your wings.
—Psalm 36:7

And so we know and rely on the love God has for us.
—1 John 4:16

Bad days are good days when
you know that you are loved
by a friend.

A friend loves at all times.
—Proverbs 17:17 NKJV

*You are my friends when you do the things I command you. I'm no
longer calling you servants because servants don't understand what
their master is thinking and planning. No, I've named you friends
because I've let you in on everything I've heard from the Father.*
—John 15:14–15 The Message

It's a good day when you know
you love someone too!

*Above all, love each other deeply, because love covers over a
multitude of sins.*
—1 Peter 4:8

Love is patient, love is kind.
—1 Corinthians 13:4

It's a good day when you enjoy
large and small happenings in life
and count them as gifts.

Every desirable and beneficial gift comes out of heaven. The gifts are
rivers of light cascading down from the Father of Light.
—James 1:17 The Message

You make known to me the path of life; in your presence there is
fullness of joy; at your right hand are pleasures forevermore.
—Psalm 16:11 ESV

It's a good day when you can enjoy
the wonderful gifts
that come your way
as a taste of good things to come.

*For behold, I create new heavens and a new earth . . . be glad and
rejoice forever in what I create.*
—Isaiah 65:17–18 NKJV

*Jesus spoke to them . . . saying: "The kingdom of heaven is like a king
who prepared a wedding banquet for his son."*
—Matthew 22:1–2

It's a good day when you know
that God has promised us His presence,
that one day we will be with Him,
and that He will share with us
all good things.

No eye has seen, nor ear heard, nor the heart of man imagined, what
God has prepared for those who love him.
—1 Corinthians 2:9 ESV

Creation itself will be liberated from its bondage to decay and brought
into the glorious freedom of the children of God.
—Romans 8:21

It's a good day when you know
that God is all about making
all things
NEW!

Behold, I will create new heavens and a new earth.
    —Isaiah 65:17

Behold, I make all things new.
    —Revelation 21:5 NKJV

*Therefore, if anyone is in Christ, he is a new creation. The old has
passed away; behold, the new has come.*
    —2 Corinthians 5:17 ESV

On days we're battered and confounded
by circumstances and people,
it's a very good day
when we seek God's direction
and follow His promptings.

I don't think the way you think. The way you work isn't the way I work . . . For as the sky soars high above earth, so the way I work surpasses the way you work.
   —Isaiah 55:8–9 The Message

Trust in the LORD with all your heart; do not depend on your own understanding. Seek his will in all you do, and he will show you which path to take.
   —Proverbs 3:5–6 NLT

If any of you lacks wisdom, let him ask of God, who gives to all liberally and without reproach, and it will be given to him.
   —James 1:5 NKJV

It's a good day when you know
some days are good
and some days not so much
and you're okay with that—
because you know
that God is good
and you trust Him.

For I have learned to be content whatever the circumstances . . .
[and whatever the] situation.
　—Philippians 4:11–12

And so we know and rely on the love God has for us.
　—1 John 4:16

Even when you're uncertain
about everything else in life,
it's a good day when
you are certain about God,
His promises,
His goodness,
His purposes,
and His plans.

*Now faith is being sure of what we hope for and certain of what we do
not see. This is what the ancients were commended for.*
    —Hebrews 11:1–2

Even on days when you sense
trouble and evil
all around you,
it's a good day when you know
that God's justice, righteousness,
and kindness will prevail.

"But let him who boasts boast about this: that he understands and knows me, that I am the LORD, who exercises kindness, justice and righteousness on earth, for in these I delight," declares the LORD.
—Jeremiah 9:24

Some days you feel like giving up,
but it's a good day
when you persevere in doing right,
in praying,
and in faith.

Wait for the Lord; be strong, and let your heart take courage; wait for the Lord!
—Psalm 27:14 ESV

So do not throw away your confidence; it will be richly rewarded.
—Hebrews 10:35–36

Don't burn out; keep yourselves fueled and aflame. Be alert servants of the Master, cheerfully expectant. Don't quit in hard times; pray all the harder.
—Romans 12:11–12 The Message

Even when you stand alone,
God counts it a good day
when you do all you can
to live in His righteousness
and you seek His kingdom.

But seek first his kingdom and his righteousness, and all these things will be given to you as well.
   —Matthew 6:33

Therefore be imitators of God, as beloved children.
   —Ephesians 5:1 ESV

For the kingdom of God is . . . righteousness and peace and joy in the Holy Spirit.
   —Romans 14:17 NKJV

It's a good day when you know
that God wants to and will
bring good things out of the bad
and blessings out of sufferings
for those
who trust in Him.

*And we know that all things work together for good to those who love
God.*
   —Romans 8:28 NKJV

It's a good day when you know
that God is for us
and
you have a small understanding
of how much He loves you
and desires to bless you.

The LORD bless you and keep you; the LORD make his face shine upon you and be gracious to you; the LORD turn his face toward you and give you peace.
　　—Numbers 6:24–26

The same Lord is Lord of all and richly blesses all who call on him, for, "Everyone who calls on the name of the Lord will be saved."
　　—Romans 10:12–13

Good Days with Evidence & Blessings

May the verses on the following pages encourage you in
God's goodness, evidence and blessings.

God's proof that He provides for us—concerning Himself, creation,
and His plans—is especially needed in tough times. His evidence
is given to guide us, strengthen us, answer our questions, and give
us hope—all of which make our days good.

Our hope is that these verses (divided in two sections—one on
evidence and one on blessings), drive you to investigate God's Word
further so that you, too, might be strengthened in God's good plans
and His extraordinary promises and provisions.

He who forms the mountains . . . reveals his thoughts to man.
—Amos 4:13

Good Days and Evidence

"I am GOD, the only God you've had or ever will have—incomparable, irreplaceable—From the very beginning telling you what the ending will be, All along letting you in on what is going to happen, Assuring you, 'I'm in this for the long haul, I'll do exactly what I set out to do'. . . I've planned it, so it's as good as done."
    —Isaiah 46:10–11 The Message

Only I can tell you the future before it even happens. Everything I plan will come to pass.
    —Isaiah 46:10 NLT

Now [they] were of more noble character . . . for they received the message with great eagerness and examined the Scriptures every day to see if what Paul said was true.
    —Acts 17:11

Do not treat prophecies with contempt. Test everything. Hold on to the good.
    —1 Thessalonians 5:20–21

Good Days and Evidence

I bring you good news of great joy that will be for all the people. Today in the town of David a Savior has been born to you; he is Christ the Lord. This will be a sign to you: You will find a baby wrapped in cloths and lying in a manger.
    —Luke 2:10–12

Believe me when I say that I am in the Father and the Father is in me; or at least believe on the evidence of the miracles themselves.
    —John 14:11

God also testified to [this great salvation] by signs, wonders and various miracles.
    —Hebrews 2:4

He has given proof of this to all men by raising [Christ Jesus] from the dead.
    —Acts 17:31

Good Days and Blessings

"For I know the plans I have for you," declares the LORD, "plans to prosper you and not to harm you, plans to give you hope and a future."
   —Jeremiah 29:11

For with the LORD there is mercy, and with him is plenteous redemption.
   —Psalm 130:7 KJV

And so we know and rely on the love God has for us.
   —1 John 4:16

I tell you the truth, whoever hears my word and believes him who sent me has eternal life and will not be condemned; he has crossed over from death to life.
   —John 5:24

Good Days and Blessings

Blessed are they whose transgressions are forgiven, whose sins are covered. Blessed is the man whose sin the Lord will never count against him.
    —Romans 4:7–8

The LORD is faithful to all his promises and loving toward all he has made.
    —Psalm 145:13

Jesus spoke to them . . . saying: "The kingdom of heaven is like a king who prepared a wedding banquet for his son."
    —Matthew 22:1–2

May you be blessed by the LORD, the Maker of heaven and earth.
    —Psalm 115:15

We hope "It's A Good Day" has inspired and strengthened you. We'd love for you to visit our websites and share how it has encouraged you.

Visit Robbi at **BlessingsandGrace.com** for more on God's goodness, good plans, evidence and helpful ideas in reading the Bible.

Visit Patricia at **PatriciaWHunter.com** for more photographic glimpses of God's glory and for cultivating an eye towards His goodness and mercy.

Encouraged by *It's a Good Day?*

For more books to share:

Ask your local retailer
or
order more at TheGoodDayBook.com.

Wholesale, bulk orders, and discount purchases available.

*May you grow in
God's good plans,
grace,
and blessings!*